293 Renaissance Woodcuts

for Artists and Illustrators

𝕵𝖔𝖘𝖙 𝕬𝖒𝖒𝖆𝖓'𝖘 𝕶𝖚𝖓𝖘𝖙𝖇𝖚̈𝖈𝖍𝖑𝖎𝖓

WITH A NEW INTRODUCTION BY ALFRED WERNER

DOVER PUBLICATIONS, INC., NEW YORK

Published in Canada by General Publishing Company, Ltd.,
30 Lesmill Road, Don Mills, Toronto, Ontario.
Published in the United Kingdom by Constable and Company,
Ltd., 10 Orange Street, London WC 2.

293 Renaissance Woodcuts for Artists and Illustrators, first
published in 1968, is an unabridged and unaltered republication of
Jost Amman's *Kunstbüchlin*, as published by Johann Feyerabend,
Frankfurt a. M., in 1599. The Introduction, written specially for
the present edition by Alfred Werner, includes new translations
of all the original German text. The captions and list of illustrations have also been prepared specially for this edition.

DOVER *Pictorial Archive* SERIES

International Standard Book Number: 0-486-21987-9
Library of Congress Catalog Card Number: 68-14561

MANUFACTURED IN THE UNITED STATES OF AMERICA
Dover Publications, Inc.
180 Varick Street
New York, N.Y. 10014

DJ21679

Introduction to the Dover Edition

Once upon a time Nuremberg (Nürnberg in German), whose proud name became the victim of its associations a few decades ago, was one of the outstanding cities of the Holy Roman Empire. In its Golden Age—around 1500—it was one of the richest and most influential of the Free Imperial Cities, an intermediary between North and South, East and West. Its manufactured goods were in such high demand that a proverb ran, "Nuremberg's hand goes through every land." Its prosperity is attested to by the fifteenth-century humanist Aeneas Sylvius (later Pope Pius II), according to whom a simple burgher of Nuremberg was better lodged than the King of Scotland. The sixteenth-century political philosopher Jean Bodin called it "the greatest, most famous and best ordered of all the Imperial cities."

Along with the wealth and civic welfare went a considerable interest in the sciences and arts. After extended travel the mathematician and astronomer Regiomontanus, for whom a rich Nuremberger built the Western World's first observatory, settled in the city, which he called "the center of Europe." The doggerel verse of its mastersinger, Hans Sachs, a shoemaker by training, is no longer widely read, yet his figure is well known from one of Wagner's operas. The city's medieval churches, patrician houses and sturdy fortifications were badly battered or totally destroyed by the bombs of World War II. But they have been lovingly reconstructed as potent reminders of a glorious past. Part and parcel of Western civilization are the works of Nuremberg's artists: the painter Michael Wolgemut and his great disciple Albrecht Dürer, and the sculptors Adam Krafft, Peter Vischer and Veit Stoss. Celebrated is the *Nuremberg Chronicle*, a huge volume with nearly two thousand illustrations, most of them by Wolgemut.

The opportunities Nuremberg offered to gifted men lured many young talents to the heart of Franconia. Among the most versatile who came and settled there was the Swiss Jost Amman—painter, print-maker, writer—who, like many of his contemporaries, turned his hand to a large variety of commercial ventures. His name, Amman, which has come to us in several slightly different versions (Aman, Ammann, Ammon—as on the title page of our *Kunstbüchlin*), was very common in the German parts of Switzerland (biographical dictionaries, incidentally, list several Ammans who were artists), and is derived from the word *Amtsmann*, magistrate. Born in Zurich on June 13, 1539, and given the name of Jodocus (which became Jos, Jost or Jobst), he was the son of a distinguished professor of logic, rhetoric, Latin and Greek who Latin-ized his name to "Ammianus." An older brother of Jost was a gold-smith. We have no certain knowledge of Jost's years of study. It is believed that his early journeys took him to the city of Basel. From there he went to Nuremberg about 1561.

Jost may have been a disciple of Virgil Solis, one of Nuremberg's most successful book illustrators. In 1562, when Solis, at the age of forty-eight, succumbed to the plague, Jost took his place as the chief artist of the famous Frankfurt printer and publisher Sigmund Feyerabend (1528–1590). Apparently Jost retained his ties to Zurich until 1574, the year of his marriage to Barbara Wilke, widow of a Nuremberg goldsmith. He now obtained the Nuremberg city council's permission to have his *aigenen Rauch* (meaning his own hearth) in "a jewel of a house" on the Obere Schmiedgasse. Though he may not have liked re-linquishing his Zurich citizenship—his early drawings are proudly signed V.Z. (i.e., from Zurich) after his initials—legal and financial advantages may have influenced him to seek naturalization in the Free Imperial City. Not only was he granted it, in 1577; he did not even have to pay the usual fee: the city was proud to adopt so "famous" and "excellent" a "painter" and "designer of copperplate engravings."

His life appears to have been without any dramatic events. His journey to Venice is merely a matter of speculation (based on a woodcut of a *festa* on the Grand Canal). All his documented trips were short ones. He traveled to Augsburg to execute a commission for the famous Fugger family; to Heidelberg, to draw the likeness of the Elector on his death bed; to the town of Altdorf (not far from Nuremberg), where he gave instruction in drawing to an elderly English nobleman; and to Frankfurt (on the Main), residence of his publisher Feyerabend. Barbara, who had borne him four children, died early in 1586. His second wife, whom he married toward the end of the same year, was also a widow, Elisabeth Maler. Though we know little about his private life—in contrast to that of Dürer, whose activities are well recorded—we must assume that his contacts with the poet Hans Sachs (with whom he collaborated on the book *Beschreybung aller Stände*) and the goldsmith Wenzel Jamnitzer, as well as with several local patricians, were not confined to business transactions, but were also personally cordial. A well-educated man, Amman was the author of a book dealing with poetry, painting and architecture. It is said that, devoid of shrewdness and toughness as he was, Amman was scandalously exploited by his chief, the rich Feyerabend. At the age of fifty-two he died rather poor, leaving a pittance to his widow and his two daughters (his two sons had passed away earlier). He was buried on March 17, 1591, but we do not know where.

Repeatedly, Amman is recorded as a *Maler* (painter). It is possible that in his youth he painted on glass, yet none of his juvenilia have come down to us. Of his oil paintings, only one, a portrait, appears to have survived; it is now in the art museum at Basel. His chief activity consisted of *Reissen*, drawing, and in documents he is referred to as a *Kunstreisser*, an artistic draftsman. Joachim von Sandrart, in his chronicle of artists, *Teutsche Akademie der edlen Bau-, Bild- und Malereikünste*, published many decades after Amman's demise, quotes one of Jost's disciples, the Frankfurt painter Jörg Keller, as saying that in the four years in which Jörg had been apprenticed to Amman, the master had produced such an enormous quantity of drawings that a hay wagon would hardly have sufficed to carry them off. While it sounds like an exaggeration—which it very well may have been—this statement confirms Jost's main area of occupation.

The graphic departments of museums in Nuremberg, Munich, Berlin, Dresden, Vienna and other cities treasure a large number of Amman's drawings, many of which are tinted with watercolor. Among them are several illustrated pedigrees of patrician families. Of special interest is Amman's documentation of Emperor Maximilian II's entry into

Nuremberg in 1570: on a series of connected leaves, in a band only fourteen and a half inches high, yet fifteen feet long, more than four hundred and fifty persons and animals are depicted.

Of even greater importance are Amman's contributions to the art of copperplate engraving and especially to the woodcut. There are single sheets, as well as books with different texts or no particular text at all. Noteworthy are his illustrations for a Bible, Livy's *History of Rome*, Josephus Flavius' *Jewish War*, *Reynard the Fox* and books on hunting, warfare, cooking and women's clothes.

Before mentioning Amman's most popular works, we might ask at this point: did he do his own engraving in wood or metal, or did he make only the drawings, which were handed over to a professional *Form-schneyder* for execution? In the sixteenth century, the woodcut, in particular, was not the personal sort of art it is today. Judging by the magnitude of Amman's output, it is not likely that he did the actual cutting, except on rare occasions; it may be assumed that he left this long, tedious task to specialized craftsmen. We know that he had the ability to do this cutting, and at least once Amman's initials are accompanied both by a quill pen and by a wood engraver's knife, clearly denoting that he himself cut the subject in addition to designing it. (In the *Kunstbüchlin*, the initials IA, for Jost Amman, can be found here and there, and at times also those of the artisan associated with the master.)

The most celebrated of the books Amman illustrated, the *Eygentliche Beschreybung aller Stände auf Erden* (1568), contains pictures of both "Der Reisser" (the draftsman) and "Der Formschneyder" (the wood engraver), which seem to be of the same individual (assumed to be a self-portrait, and probably used as model for a portrait drawing of Amman made in the middle of the seventeenth century by Erhard Dürsteler. This *Beschreybung* contains well over a hundred descriptions of people in a variety of professions and occupations, from Pope, Cardinal, Bishop and Emperor down to the lowest, the Fool. Most of the illustrations deal with the crafts of artisans, and they are patiently rendered with so much accuracy that the artist must have drawn them from life, sparing no pains to get the details right. Under each picture is a short poem by Hans Sachs (1494–1576) commenting on the particular person and his calling. Apart from the fact that this book provides a pictorial record of late sixteenth-century culture in its customs and costumes, tools and techniques, it is also a sheer delight to the eye. The *Beschreybung* was reprinted many times, and even appeared with a Latin text. Since the original books soon became collectors' items— prior to 1800, editions were extremely small, by our standards— facsimile editions were produced in modern Germany. Individual pictures from the book appear repeatedly in works dealing with the period, and also in histories of graphic art.

An equally rare title is the volume now reprinted, the *Kunstbüchlin*. This is the fourth edition of an Amman work first published by Sigmund Feyerabend in 1578, in Latin and German versions. The German title of the first edition was *Kunst und Lehrbüchlein für die anfahenden Jungen Daraus reissen und Malen zu lernen Darinnen allerley Art lustige und artliche fürreissung von Manns und Weibsbildern Desgleichen von Kindlein Thierlein und anderen stücklein. Allen liebhabenden Jungen dieser Kunst zum besten an tag geben* (Art and instruction book for young beginners, from which to learn how to draw and paint; containing all sorts of cheerful and pleasant illustrations of men and women, also of little children, little animals and other subjects; published for the benefit of all young people who love this art). The fourth edition, considerably enlarged by the inclusion of pictures that had appeared earlier in other books illustrated by Amman, was issued by the house of Feyerabend in 1599, after the demise of both the artist and the founder of the firm.

The 1599 edition is no longer restricted to purposes of instruction; its goal is the delectation of the general book purchaser. The title page, written in the language of the early New High German period, is now a bit difficult to understand; it might be translated freely thus:

A little Book of Art, wherein are included, besides the representations of many clergymen and secular persons of high and low rank, as well as those of the Turkish Emperors and their chief men, all kinds of artistic designs and figures; also the seven planets, the ten ages; cavalry captains and commanding officers; riders and their horses; all sorts of tournaments; swordsmanship and armor. All of it most elegantly and artistically drawn by the late excellent and far renowned Jost Ammon [*sic!*]

of Nuremberg. Now again compiled and offered to all the lovers of painting, in order to please them especially.

At the bottom of the title page, underneath the picture of a fountain (one of the printer's marks of the Feyerabend firm), the imprint: "Printed at Frankfurt on the Main, 1599." Five lines of type (2, 3, 11, 13 and imprint) are in red. The angular, pointed Gothic type is used which at one time was employed extensively all over Europe; it is called *Fraktur* in German.

As was the custom, the dedication of this volume was signed in the name of the publisher,* Carl Sigmund Feyrabend [*sic!*], who was a relative of the late founder of the firm. It was probably written by one of the starving intellectuals employed as hacks, as it is in the stilted language of a German humanist, with allusions to Latin literature. Freely translated, the dedication is headed:

To the noble, severe and honorable Octavius von Straden zu Rossburg, citizen of the Roman Empire, noble courtier of Emperor Rudolph II and antiquary, my particularly kindly inclined Lord.

And then it goes on in a manner which was fashionable four centuries ago:

Noble, honorable and kindly inclined Lord and Friend: The highly renowned orator Cicero wrote, after considering how a man should spend his lifetime in a useful and praiseworthy manner, that whoever wishes to leave behind a good name must above all see to it that he leave behind something useful and profitable to the common fatherland, considering that he was not born to spend his life in laziness and inertia— which might fairly be called one of the greatest vices—but that as much as it is possible for him, he should serve the common good in some manner; just as in the past the ancients considered this to be the highest good, for which one must aim in this life with all earnestness, as such records of antiquity as still can be found testify sufficiently. Moreover, the more they benefited the common good the more honor was given to them, and many of them were even elevated to divinity by the ancient pagans and honored by them. Although this is not strictly proper, one may nonetheless deduce from it how they held in high esteem those who

---

* In this case apparently a member of the publisher's family, since the colophon on the last page of the book names Johann Feyrabend as publisher (and Romanus Beatus as printer).

had done something memorable. Therefore, when the present *Kunstbuch* came to my attention, I could easily discern that if it were published it would result in profit and benefit, as well as in especial pleasure, to many, since not only are many varied things illustrated in it, but also a great deal of industry and art have been used in all the figures, so that we can look at them with greater delight and also imitate them. Since I am far from unaware of the pleasure my Lord finds in this art (indeed, not long ago at my Lord's house I myself saw the profusion [of art works]), I have been strongly induced by this (on account of the many favors which he has bestowed on me and as a further testimony to our friendship) to dedicate this *Kunstbüchlin* to my Lord, hoping without any doubt that my Lord will, as a special lover of the arts, receive and accept it in his patronage and protection, and will permit me to consider myself his friend, as before. With this I commend myself to the grace of God. Given in Frankfurt on the Main, on the last day of August, in the year 1599.

The always most obedient servant of my Lord,
Carl Sigmund Feyrabend.

Following this dedication/preface are 293 illustrations, plus a colophon ornament, all in woodcut. The Gothic letters below certain pictures, often followed by Roman numbers (e.g., A, Aii, Aiii), are guides for the printer rather than information for the purchaser of the little book.

In addition to the pictures originally drawn for the 1578 *Kunst und Lehrbüchlein* (chiefly the pictures of women and children, the bishops, the allegories and the pagan gods), the *Kunstbüchlin* contains illustrations (generally identifiable by subject matter) from two 1577 works on Turkey, *Das Leben Scanderbegs* (The Life of Scanderbeg) by Marinus Barletius, translated into German by Johannes Pinicianus, and *Türckische Chronica*, translated by Heinrich Müller; from the 1579 *Stam und Wapenbuch hochs und niders Standts* (Book of pedigrees and coats-of-arms of high and low degree); from the 1581 *Ein newes Kochbuch* (A new cookbook) by Marx Rumpolt (the illustrations 252–257 are from this book); from the two 1584 works *Ritterliche Reutterkunst* (Knightly horsemanship) by L. V. C. and *Von der Gestüterey* (On horse breeding) by Marx Fugger (second edition of a 1578 work); and other books issued by the firm of Feyerabend.

In the *Kunstbüchlin* there is no strict logical order in the arrangement of the illustrations, although there are rough groupings by subject matter or earlier sources.* Many of the pictures are inspired by stories of ancient mythology, such as those of the brothers Romulus and Remus protected by the she-wolf, Venus and Amor, Hercules, Neptune, Ganymede, Bacchus, Mars, Jupiter, Diana and other pagan deities who, if not in the nude, wear the lush costumes of the late sixteenth century, or what is supposed to have been ancient Greek clothing. The female nude is astonishingly frequent, as are women whose apparel suggests rather than conceals the body's charms. Of course, it must be borne in mind that the Gothic Age, which made a sharp distinction between body and soul, physical and spiritual beauty, and which frowned on nudity and even on any display of sensuality, had by 1599 been superseded in the German lands by the Renaissance and the early Baroque. With the neo-pagan interests frequent among humanists, there was a trend toward a hearty lasciviousness, toward an audacious and even frivolous world-liness, and whatever Amman's personal attitude was in this matter, he offered what his patrons wanted: large-breasted, large-hipped Venuses in suggestive poses.

Contemporary buyers of this book also liked to see fashionably dressed men or women on fine horses—they appear here approximately ninety times. Apparently, art patrons loved examples of high living, and in these plates there is often such emphasis on precious and elaborate costume at the expense of facial expression that at times the figures look as though they had been inserted into the clothing as an after-thought—as though they were little more than mannequins. At the same time, Amman's patrons—aristocrats like the knight to whom the volume is dedicated, or patricians—also enjoyed seeing, from a safe distance, how the "common people" lived, and how much inferior they were. This explains the appeal in the sixteenth century (and thereafter)

---

* The original edition of the *Kunstbüchlin* had no illustration numbers or captions. The captions (and list of plates) in the present edition are based on the identifications of the subjects to be found in the two most extensive catalogues of Amman's works: C[arl] Becker, *Jobst Amman, Zeichner und Formschneider, Kupferätzer und Stecher*, Rudolph Weigel, Leipzig, 1854 (the *Kunstbüchlin* is catalogue number 27d in Becker); and Andreas Andresen, *Der deutsche Peintre-Graveur oder die deutschen Maler als Kupferstecher*, Rudolph Weigel, Leipzig, 1864, Vol. I (the *Kunstbüchlin* is under catalogue number 237 in Andresen).

of *genre* art not concerned with social questions and totally devoid of
social criticism. Hence the many plates showing stable boys, farmers
and other representatives of "low life," often with a comic note.

Death turns up once or twice, in the traditional shape of a skeleton,
but he is not a really frightening sight. There is an occasional tree, and
now and then landscape is used as a background, decades after landscape had been developed as an independent motif first by Dürer and
then by Altdorfer. Amman was no nature lover like Altdorfer. Nor was
he a deeply religious man with a metaphysical bent, like Dürer. In this
Kunstbüchlin, the world of the Bible is sparsely represented, with
pictures of Elijah fed by the ravens, Judith with the head of Holofernes,
the Evangelists and a few other such subjects. Instead, we find many
pictures of Turks, officers, riders, hunters, mothers with babies, peasants
and a variety of well-fed little angels, some of them making music.
Many decorations for escutcheons are shown (with the escutcheon itself
blank). The escutcheon is sometimes flanked by two persons, a man and
a woman.

While a remarkable craftsman, Amman was not a lonely genius,
driven by his inner *daimon*, like Dürer. Dürer was an innovator who—
as we know from some of his utterances—felt ill at ease in what has been
dubbed the "German Athens" or the "Florence of the North," because
the Nurembergers, who gave ample employment to tradition-bound
artists, were distrustful of novelty and even put a brake on strong
individualists. Notwithstanding the activities of Dürer and other men
of genius, the affluent city preferred middle-of-the-roaders and had a
rather pragmatic approach to art. As one of its historians, Gerald
Strauss, put it, "In Nuremberg culture was valued only if it was demon-
strably useful and practical, and if it added material value or enjoyment
of life. Thus the arts which flourished best were those that offered
something of instruction or delight to people of ordinary tastes"
(*Nuremberg in the sixteenth century*, 1966).

Amman was their man! This *Kunstbüchlin* filled the purpose served
in our time by often far more opulent illustrated books—to give pleasure,
but also all kinds of information, to the eyes of those leafing through it.
Undoubtedly, it was also used as a source book for illustrators and
decorators who would copy or adapt details or even whole compositions.

Amman's age was one that liked theatricality and a smiling art with an emphasis on animated movement and dynamic curves, and with a love for accessories and furnishings of all sorts rather than Gothic angularity and austerity. Amman supplied what was wanted: figures which, while static, give the illusion of movement; bodies conceived three-dimensionally within a unified spatial perspective; images rich in variety, all details being shown with unsurpassed precision. What we have here, then, is the work of a virtuoso apparently without any inner drive, an artist willing to lend his enormous gifts to the requirements of supply and demand so as to enable himself to live with a modicum of comfort, and to clothe and feed his family. There is no expressionistic *Sturm und Drang*; instead, there is the hedonistic entertainment which we also find elsewhere in the ages of Mannerism and the early Baroque.

There are no profound moral or religious lessons in this book. There is no high-keyed emotionalism. But there is instruction and the delight of playfulness. Amman was no Dürer, yet he was an eminent figure in the period when the decline was starting in the arts of Germany (which were not to recover until the early years of the present century). He might be grouped, and has, indeed, been listed among the "Little Masters" or "Small Masters"—men like Jörg Pencz, the Beham brothers and Heinrich Aldegrever—so called not, as one might think, because they were of minor significance as artists, which they were not, but because they chose to express themselves in works of rather small physical size. Whatever Amman may lack in philosophical depth, he was unquestionably a keen and clever observer of the world around him, and he was, above all, a first-rate craftsman.

It is profitable to look at his work, and to note the progress the woodcut had made, at least technically speaking, in the German lands in a dozen decades or so. In Western Europe, the first woodcuts turned up around 1400, and the technique was employed partly for religious purposes and partly for the making of playing cards. Woodcuts were issued—often anonymously—either as single sheets or as book illustrations. Blockbooks had quite a vogue in the later fifteenth century; there both text and illustrations were cut on the same wooden block, and the results were often crude, notwithstanding the master's inventiveness. About the same time there arose another procedure, in which wood blocks were used only for the illustrations, while the text was printed from movable type (as is the case in the—much later—*Kunstbüchlin*). In the making of such books at least four individuals participated: the artist who drew the design; the craftsman who cut them into the wood block; the printer who set the text; and the publisher (although in many cases the publisher and the printer were one and the same person).

The principles of the making of woodcuts have not changed much to this very day. The design is drawn, often with pen, in ink, on a piece of smooth hardwood. Then the surface on either side of the desired line is cut away, leaving the design in relief—raised and isolated from the background. Next, printer's ink is applied to this raised surface. Finally, paper is placed over it, and with pressure exerted from above, the image is transferred. But while the earliest masters of the woodcut had to confine themselves to a few, relatively thick, lines, by 1500 woodcuts were composed of hundreds of very delicate and often curved lines, and much crosshatching was employed to give figures a three-dimensionality, a roundness, lacking in the early works, which do not attempt to model by means of light and shade.

The men who worked for Amman could do everything he wanted them to do, and executed their work with astonishing diligence and neatness, but they were mere technicians without any artistic ambitions. These Amman had; for while he may have been what today is called a commercial artist, in all his years of unceasing productivity he never created anything sloppy in composition or hasty in design. To judge by the persons and things he drew, wherever he turned he found something to interest him. His eyes delighted in the plump beauty of women, the sumptuous elegance of contemporary clothing, the exciting features of tournaments, the spirited movements of horses and hounds, the activities of peasants and other people of low rank. Modern perusers of this *Kunstbüchlin* are likely to agree with Carl Sigmund Feyerabend that this little book will "result in profit and benefit, as well as in especial pleasure, to many."

New York   ALFRED WERNER
March 1968

List of Illustrations

[xvi]

Kunstbüchlin/

Darinnen neben Für-

bildung vieler/ Geistlicher vnnd Weltli-
cher/ Hohes vnd Niderstands Personen/ so dann auch
der Türckischen Käyser/ vnnd derselben Obersten/ allerhande
Kunstreiche Stück vnnd Figuren: Auch die sieben Planeten/ Zehen Al-
ter/ Rittmeister vnnd Befelchshaber/ Reuterey/ vnd Contrafactur
der Pferde/ allerley Thurnier/ Fechten/ vnd dann et-
liche Helm vnd Helmdecken be-
griffen.

Alles auff das zierlichst vnd künstlichst gerissen/ durch
weylandt den fürtrefflichen vnd weitberümbten

Jost Ammon von Nürnberg.

Jetzund von newem/ allen denen/ so der Kunst der Malerey zugethan/
vnd deren Liebhabern/ zusonderm Gefallen zusammen
verfaßt/ vnd an Tag geben.

Gedruckt zu Franckfurt am Mayn/ 1599.

Dem Edlen / Gestren-
gen / vnnd Ehrnvesten / Octavio von
Straden zů Roßburg / Ciui Romano, Rv-
DOLPHI II. Imperatoris Nobili Aulico,
vnd Antiquario, Meinem insonders günstigen Herrn.

 Dler / Ehrnvester /
Insonders Gün-
stiger Herr vnnd
Freundt / Es schrei-
bet der hochberům-
te Orator CICERO,
nachdem er bey sich
betrachtete / wie der
Mensch die Zeit seines Lebens nützlich vñ
löblich möge zubringen / Nemlich / daß ein
jeder / so da begert einē guten Namen hin-
der sich zuverlassen / vor allen dingen da-
mit vmbgehe / daß er etwas nützlichs / vnd
gemeinem Vatterland fürträgliches hin-
derlaß

derlaſſe / in Betrachtung / daß er nicht ge-
boren ſey / ſein Leben in Träg vnnd Faul-
heit zu zubringen/welches daſ der gröſten
Laſter eins billich mag genennet werden/
ſondern daß er/ ſo viel jm jmmer müglich/
mit etwas dem gemeinen Nutzen gedienet
ſeye. In maſſen dann vorzeiten die Alten
ſolches vor das Höchſte gehalten haben /
darnach man in dieſem Leben fürnemlich
mit allem Ernſt ſtreben ſolle : wie daſ die
alten Monumenta, ſo noch vnterſchiedtlich
funden werden / ſolches gnugſam bezeu-
gen. Ja zum oberfluß/je mehr ſie gemeinem Nutzen fruchtbarlichers habē erfun-
den/je höher ſie nachmals ſind geehret/Ja
auch deren viel von den alten Heyden zu
Göttern gemacht / vnd von jhnen geehret
worden. Welches / ob es wol nicht faſt al-
lerding recht/ ſo iſt doch hierauß abzunem-
men/ wie in hohem Weÿrt vnnd Anſehen
die

die jenigen / so etwas denckwürdiges auff
die Bahn bracht / bey jhnen gehalten worden. Demnach dann auch mir gegenwer-
tiges Kunstbuch vorkommen / auch leicht-
lich erachten kundte / da es an Tag bracht /
würde es vielen zu Nutz vnd Gutem / wie
dañ auch zu besonderlicher Lustierung er-
spriesen / in Erwegung / daß nicht allein
viel vnnd mancherley Sachen hierin vor-
gebildet / sondern auch ein sonderlicher
Fleiß vnnd Kunst in allen Stücken ge-
braucht / vñ dannen hero vmb so viel desto
anmuhtiger zu schauwen vnd zu imitiren
seyn werden. Nachdem mir nun nit wenig bewußt das sonderliche Wolgefallen
deß Herrn zu dieser Kunst / (wie ich dann
kurtz verruckter Zeit bey dem Herren die
Menning selbsten gesehen) bin ich nicht
wenig dardurch verursacht worden (we-
gen vieler Gutthaten / so ich empfangen /

):(iij   auch

auch zu mehrer Bestättigung vnserer
Freundtschafft) solchs Kunstbüchlin dem
Herrn zu dediciren vnd zu verehren/ vnge-
zweiffelter Hoffnung / der Herr werde es/
als ein sonderer Liebhaber der Künsten/ in
seinen Schutz vnnd Patrocinium auff vnd
an nemmen / Mich auch/ wie biß hero/ für
seinen Freundt erkennen. Hiemit vns
samptlich in die Gnade Gottes trewlich
befohlen. Actum Franckfurt am Mayn/
den letzten Augusti / Im Jahr 1599.

Deß Herrn

Dienstwilliger allezeit

Carl Sigmund Feyrabend.

1. Ten heads of men of different ages

2. Three cherubs and an angel with a lute

3. Mounted putto with a banner

4. Two putti carrying a basket of fruit

5. Two putti returning from the hunt

6. Two putti with a pot

7. Two putti with helmet and banner

8. Cupid shooting an arrow

9. Romulus and Remus with the she-wolf

10. Four putti with musical instruments

11. Woman and child

12. Venus with two amoretti

13. Woman nursing a child

14. Venus and Cupid overheard by a satyr

15. Venus and Cupid wrestling

16. Nymph on a unicorn

17. Cimon and his daughter (classical legend of young woman sustaining
her starving imprisoned father with her own milk)

18. Mars, Venus and Cupid

ℭ ij

19. Venus handing Mars a cup

20. Nymph and bagpipe-playing bear

21. Diana on a stag

22. Warrior or hunter leading a stag

23. Hunter with two dogs

24. Duck hunter

25. Curtius riding into the pit (Roman legend).

26. Hercules and the hydra

27. Hercules and the Nemean lion

28. Neptune on a "seahorse"

29. Ganymede on Jupiter's eagle

30. Bacchus on a wine vat

31. Two satyrs carrying fruit

32. Lady with a birdhouse and flying fools

33. Man with a goblet and a lady

34. Man with a goblet and lady with a wreath

35. Elijah fed by a raven

36. Three pilgrims

37. St. Jerome (or else the Evangelist Mark)

38. Judith with the head of Holofernes

39. The Evangelist Matthew

40. Judith giving the head of Holofernes to her servant

41. Musicians

42. Peasant couple embracing

43. Peasant couple dancing

44. Minerva with an owl

45. Fortune (or Venus) with a sail on a globe

46. Fame and a horse-drawn sled

47. Fame and a sled drawn by crustaceans

48. Fame and a sled drawn by crustaceans

49. Apollo as sun god

50. Diana as moon goddess

51. Mars

52. Jupiter and his eagle

53. Mercury with shield and caduceus

54. Venus and Cupid

55. Saturn about to devour one of his children

56. Cybele and her dragons

57. Europa and the bull

58. Bellona with a laurel wreath

59. Siren playing a harp

60. Allegory of Justice

𝕳 iij

61. Allegory of Faith

62. Allegory of Industriousness

63. Ceres

64. Diana as huntress

65. Allegory of Geometry or Melancholy

66. Allegory of Architecture

67. Allegory of Truth

68. Allegory of Strength or Fortitude

J iij

69. Allegorical figure of woman holding a heart

70. Allegorical figure of woman holding a mask

71. Woman with a fox

72. Venus and Cupid

73. Woman playing a lute

74. Woman playing a harp

75. Woman playing a portative organ

76. Woman with a triangle

K iij

77. Flora

78. Allegory of Sculpture

79. Kneeling woman

80. Woman pouring a liquid

81. Death surprising a pair of lovers

82. A bishop

83. A bishop

84. A bishop

85. A bishop

86. A bishop

87. A bishop

88. A Turk with a scepter

89. A Turk with a saber and a scepter

90. A Turk with a scepter

91. A Turk with a scepter

92. A Turk with a short sword and a scepter

93. A Turk with a tent in the background

94. A Turk with an officer's baton

95. A Turk with shield and mace

96. A Turk with scepter and a battle-axe

97. A Turk with shield and scepter

98. A Turk with a mace

99. A Turk with a scepter

100. A Turk with shield and scepter

N iij

101. A Hungarian with a mace

102. Soldier with a spear

103. Warrior in armor with shield and mace

104. Ensign carrying flag with lion

105. Ensign carrying flag with Burgundian cross

106. Military drummer

107. A landsknecht

108. Sleeping woman with child and animals

109. A landsknecht

110. Landsknecht with rooster

111. Military drummer

112. Dueler with quarterstaff

113. Dueler with quarterstaff

114. Dueler with two-handed sword (*en garde* position)

𝔓 ij

115. Dueler with two-handed sword (*en garde* position)

116. Dueler with short sword (dusack)

117. Dueler with short sword (dusack)

118. Four schoolchildren

119. Man with a bumper; lovers in background

120. Hunter; horseman firing pistol in background

121. Warrior in armor; jouster in background

122. Merchant; port scene in background

123. Merchant; fox with a fowl

124. Man with a rosary; two men at board game

125. Old man with cat

126. Old man with crutch; horse in background

127. Old man and Death

128. Girl with doll and two other children

129. Woman and lutenist

130. Woman with peacock

131. Mother and daughter; hen on eggs

132. Old woman with crane

R lij

133. Old woman with swan

134. Old woman with eagle

135. Old woman with owl

136. Old woman with bat

137. Old woman with Death

138. Cavalryman with whip

139. Mounted bugler

140. Cavalryman with pistol

141. Cavalryman with pistol

142. Cavalryman

143. Cavalryman with short cape

144. Cavalryman

145. Cavalryman with staling horse

146. Mounted drummer

147. Mounted bugler

148. Two cavalrymen with muskets

149. Two cavalrymen with muskets

150. Two cavalrymen with spears

151. Two cavalrymen with spears

152. Cavalryman

153. Cavalryman with officer's baton

154. Two professors (*doctores*) on horseback

V ij

155. Mounted professor (*doctor*) with switch

156. An Elector of the Empire on horseback with drawn sword

157. An Elector of the Empire on horseback with switch

158. The Holy Roman Emperor on horseback

159. The "Roman King" (King of Germany) on horseback

160. An Elector of the Empire on horseback

161. The Count Palatine on horseback

162. A Spanish horseman

163. Horseman with a falcon

164. Two Hungarian cavalrymen

165. A Hungarian cavalryman

166. Cavalryman with spear

167. Hungarian cavalryman with staff

168. Cavalryman with battle-axe

169. Turkish cavalryman with pennant

170. Turkish cavalryman with bow and arrows

171. Two Turkish cavalrymen

172. Cavalryman

173. Cavalryman

174. Cavalryman

175. Cavalryman with mace

176. Cavalryman

177. Cavalryman with short cape

178. Cavalryman

179. Cavalryman; infantryman in background

180. Cavalryman with crossbow

181. Cavalryman

182. Cavalryman

183. Cavalryman with long cape

184. Cavalryman with spear

185. Cavalryman leading a riderless horse

186. Horseman

187. Three peasants on horseback

188. Peasant with four horses

189. Mounted peasant leading a riderless horse

190. Lady on horseback holding a branch

191. Lady on horseback holding a fan

192. Lady on horseback holding a switch

193. Lady on horseback holding a switch

194. Man and lady on one horse

195. Lady on horseback

196. Man on horseback and standing lady

197. Man and lady on horseback

198. Horse with plumes in its mane

199. Horse with rich trappings

200. Horse

201. Horse with rich trappings

202. Horse rearing on its hind legs

203. Horse

204. Horse hitched to a post

205. Horse rearing on its forelegs

206. Horse, with rider, dragging a load

207. Two men, one leading a horse

208. A laden horse

209. Peasant pasturing horses

210. Horse and groom

211. Man preparing horse medicine in a mortar

212. Horses in a field

Dd iij

213. Three horses

214. Stable scene

215. Peasant with donkeys (or mules)

216. Horse being shod

217. Horse being given medicine through a funnel

218. Horse being branded

Ee ij

219. Horse being bled

220. Man leading a lame horse

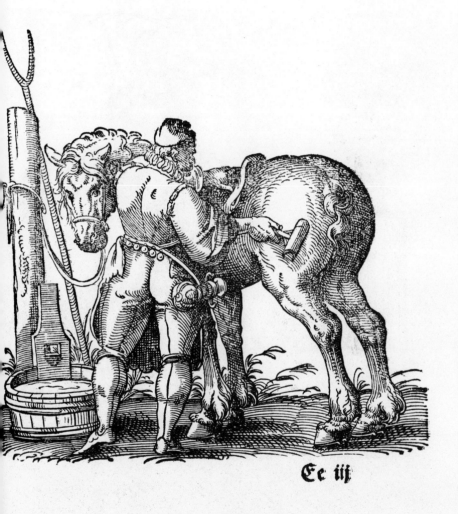

221. Horse being currycombed

222. Sick horse; horseman in background

223. Knight with lance

224. Knight with lance

225. Cavalryman with lance

226. Knight with lance

227. Jouster with lance

228. Jouster with lance

Ff iij

229. Jouster with lance

230. Jousters with lances

231. Jousters with lances

232. Jousters with lances

233. Jousters with lances

Gg

234. Jousters with lance and sword

235. Jousters with lance and sword

Gg ij

236. Jousters with lances

237. Equestrian combat with swords

Gg iij

238. Equestrian combat with swords

239. Equestrian combat with daggers

240. Equestrian combat with swords

241. Equestrian combat with lance and dagger

242. Equestrian combat with sword and dagger

248. Equestrian combat with hook

Hh ii

244. Equestrian combat with noose

245. Equestrian combat hand to hand

H iii

246. Equestrian combat hand to hand

247. Equestrian combat hand to hand

248. Cambyses of Persia on the judge's seat beneath the flayed skin of
the corrupt judge Sisamnes

249. Dying man surveying his treasures

250. Men counting money and treasures

251. Two burghers in conversation

252. Two burghers in conversation

Ji iij

253. Two burghers, one counting out money into the other's hand

254. Two burghers, one giving the other a double bumper

255. Two burghers in conversation

256. Two burghers in conversation

257. Two burghers in conversation

258. Gentleman and lady and old man with double bumper

259. Courtroom scene

260. Blank escutcheon; ensign

261. Blank escutcheon; Minerva

262. Blank escutcheon; knight with officer's baton

263. Blank escutcheon; knight with officer's baton

264. Blank escutcheon; woman with banner

265. Blank escutcheon; knight with halberd

266. Blank escutcheon; woman with jug and bowl

Ll ij

267. Blank escutcheon; military officer

268. Blank escutcheon; woman with mirror (allegory of Truth?)

269. Blank escutcheon; knight with pistol and staff

270. Blank escutcheon; wild man and woman

271. Blank escutcheon; young man and woman

272. Blank escutcheon; gentleman with goblet and lady

273. Blank escutcheon; woman and knight

274. Blank escutcheon; young man and woman

275. Blank escutcheon; woman with branch

276. Blank escutcheon; lady

277. Blank escutcheon; man playing lute

278. Blank escutcheon; lady

279. Blank escutcheon; half-nobleman, half-cleric

280. Blank escutcheon; nude woman with monkey

Nn

281. Blank escutcheon; knight with two-handed sword

282. Blank escutcheon; lady

283. Blank escutcheon; lady

284. Blank escutcheon; allegory of Faith

Nn iii

285. Blank escutcheon; lady with short cape

286. Blank escutcheon

287. Blank escutcheon

288. Blank escutcheon; woman with the Serpent and the Cross

289. Blank escutcheon; man with a bumper

290. Blank escutcheon; man with flute and woman with hurdygurdy

291. Blank escutcheon; nude woman with hedgehog

292. Winged ox (symbol of St. Luke?) with coat-of-arms

293. Blank escutcheon

Getruckt zu Franckfurt am Mayn,
durch Romanum Beatum/ in Verle-
gung Johann Feyrabends.

1 5 9 9